Why the Oyster Has the Pearl

by Johnette Downing

illustrated by Bethanne Hill

PELICAN PUBLISHING COMPANY
Gretna 2011

The word "Pelican" and the depiction of a pelican are
trademarks of Pelican Publishing Company, Inc., and are
registered in the U.S. Patent and Trademark Office.

Library of Congress Cataloging-in-Publication Data

Downing, Johnette.
  Why the oyster has the pearl / written by Johnette Downing ; illustrated by Bethanne Hill.
    p. cm.
  Summary: Explains why oysters make pearls and dangerous snakes have diamond-shaped heads.
  ISBN 978-1-4556-1460-8 (hardcover : alk. paper) [1. Oysters—Fiction. 2. Snakes—Fiction. 3. Greed—Fiction.] I. Hill, Bethanne, ill. II. Title.
  PZ7.D759277Wh 2011
  [E]—dc23

                                        2011012263

Printed in Singapore
Published by Pelican Publishing Company, Inc.
1000 Burmaster Street, Gretna, Louisiana 70053

Why the Oyster has the Pearl

In the beginning, the Oyster was the
keeper of all of the jewels in the world.

The Oyster was generous and kind. He would display the jewels for any creature who wanted to see them and would give jewels to any creature who needed them.

Of all of the Snakes in the world, there was one who was greedy. As he watched many creatures visit the Oyster, the Snake was scheming.

"Oh, dear Oyster," he said. "I've seen all of the creatures in the great water. They sparkle with the colors of the jewels you have given them. My eyesight is poor. Would you give me two emeralds for my eyes, to help me see?"

"Sure," said the Oyster. "Choose the ones you need and leave the rest." The Snake picked the two largest emeralds he could find, placed them on his eyes, and swam away.

The following day, the Snake returned to the Oyster. "Oh, gracious Oyster, the emeralds you gave me for my eyes are green like the sea. Everything I look upon is green. I can't tell one thing from another. May I have four amethysts to help reflect the sun's rays and help me see better?"

"Sure," said the Oyster. "Choose the ones you need and leave the rest." The Snake took the four brightest amethysts he could find, placed them over the emeralds in his eyes, and swam away.

The following day, the Snake returned to the Oyster. "Oh, gentle Oyster, my tongue is forked and drab. Nothing tastes good on my tongue. Perhaps you can spare a ruby or two or ten to make my tongue a deep, delicious red?" "Sure," said the Oyster. "Choose the ones you need and leave the rest." The Snake slurped up every ruby in sight with his long tongue and swam away.

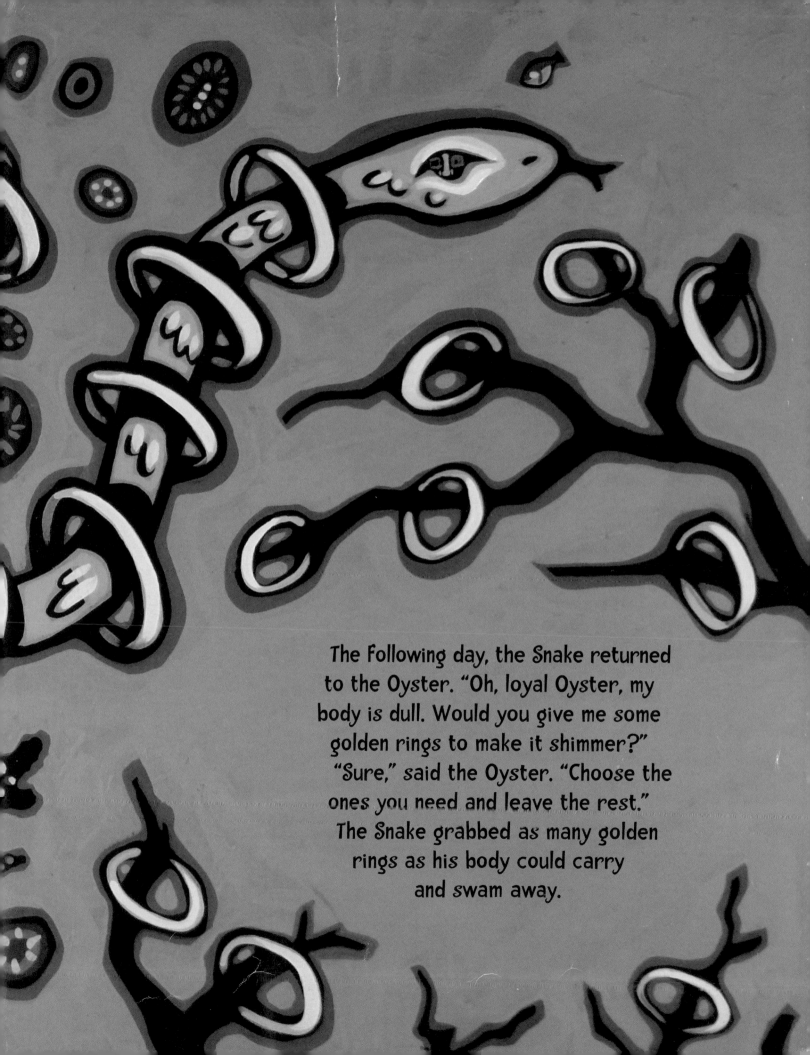

The following day, the Snake returned to the Oyster. "Oh, loyal Oyster, my body is dull. Would you give me some golden rings to make it shimmer?"
"Sure," said the Oyster. "Choose the ones you need and leave the rest."
The Snake grabbed as many golden rings as his body could carry and swam away.

The following day, the Snake returned
to the Oyster. "Oh, noble Oyster, the
golden rings you gave me are heavy
and slide off my body when I swim.
Some sapphires would be useful to
keep the golden rings in place. May I
have two or three hundred sapphires?"
"Sure," said the Oyster. "Choose the
ones you need and leave the rest."
The Snake took every last sapphire
he could find, as well as a few other
jewels, slid them between the golden
rings, and swam away.

Finally, as the sun gave way to the moon,
the Snake returned to the Oyster. "Oh, dear,
gracious, gentle, loyal, noble, and courageous
Oyster, the water is so dark when the sun sleeps.
I have no sunlight to reflect light on my eyes. I
am lost and cannot find my way home in the dark.
What could you give me to help me go home?"
The Oyster looked at his jewels. He only had two
jewels left that the Snake had not taken. "I am sorry
to say that I only have two jewels in my keeping.
Choose the one you need and leave the rest."

The Snake looked at the two jewels. There was a large sparkling diamond and a small pearl. The Snake quickly stuffed the large diamond into his mouth. Then he snatched the pearl too and crammed it into his mouth. "Ha, ha, ha, you foolish Oyster. I have swindled you out of all of your jewels. Now you have nothing."

The Snake laughed and laughed so hard that the diamond became wedged in his jaw, and the pearl became lodged in his throat. He coughed and gagged, and then he began choking. "Help! Help me, friend Oyster," gasped the Snake.

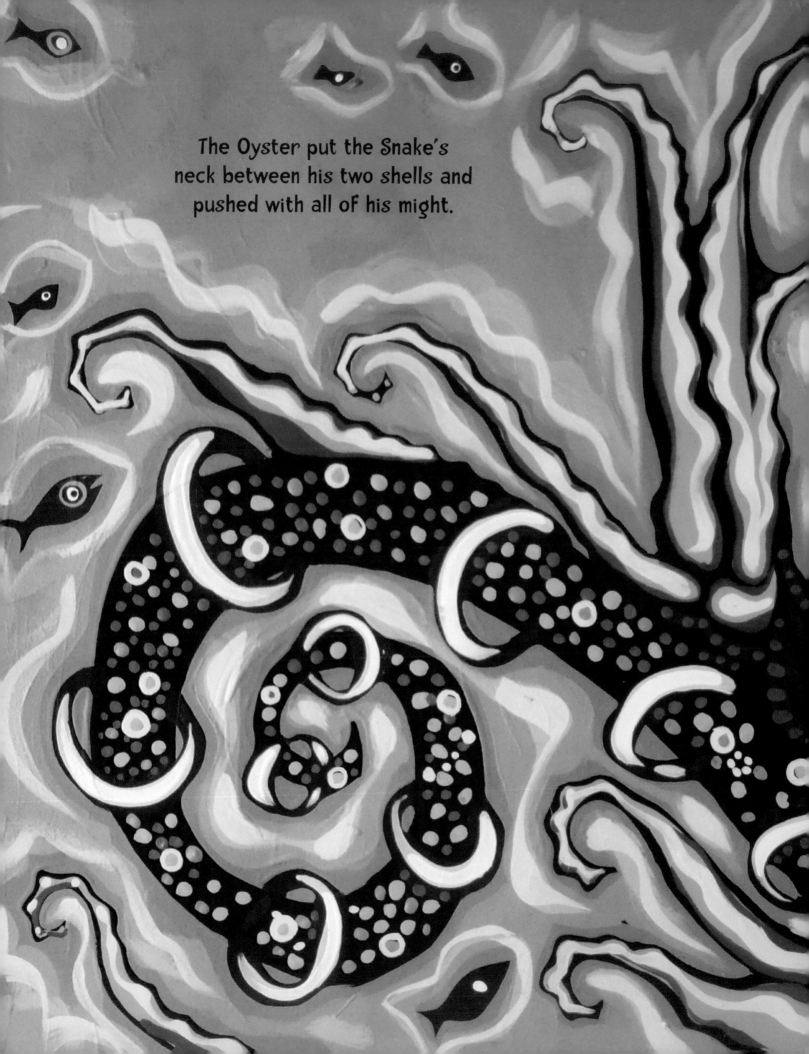

The Oyster put the Snake's neck between his two shells and pushed with all of his might.

The pearl popped out of the
Snake's throat and landed inside
the Oyster's shell. The Snake could
breathe again, but the diamond
was wedged in his jaw forever.

And that is why,
even to this day, the
Snakes who are not
to be trusted have
diamond-shaped
heads and why the
Oyster has the pearl.